YOU CHOOSE

GREAT ESCAPES

CAN YOU SURVIVE A WORLD WAR I ESCAPE?

AN INTERACTIVE HISTORY ADVENTURE

BY ERIC BRAUN

CAPSTONE PRESS
a capstone imprint

Published by Capstone Press, an imprint of Capstone
1710 Roe Crest Drive, North Mankato, Minnesota 56003
capstonepub.com

Library of Congress Cataloging-in-Publication Data
Names: Braun, Eric, 1971– author.
Title: Can you survive a World War I escape? : an interactive history adventure / by Eric Braun.
Description: North Mankato, Minnesota : Capstone Press, [2024] | Series: You choose: great escapes | Includes bibliographical references. | Audience: Ages 8–12. | Audience: Grades 4–6. | Summary: An interactive World War I adventure where the reader determines their fate during a daring escape from a prisoner-of-war camp.
Identifiers: LCCN 2023014725 (print) | LCCN 2023014726 (ebook) | ISBN 9781669061274 (hardcover) | ISBN 9781669061397 (paperback) | ISBN 9781669061311 (pdf) | ISBN 9781669061403 (epub)
Subjects: CYAC: Plot-your-own stories. | World War, 1914–1918—Fiction. | Prisoner-of-war camps—Fiction. | Escapes—Fiction. | Plot-your-own stories. | LCGFT: Choose-your-own stories. | Novels.
Classification: LCC PZ7.1.B751542 Can 2024 (print) | LCC PZ7.1.B751542 (ebook) | DDC [Fic]—dc23
LC record available at https://lccn.loc.gov/2023014725
LC ebook record available at https://lccn.loc.gov/2023014726

Editorial Credits
Editor: Christopher Harbo; Designer: Sarah Bennett; Media Researcher: Svetlana Zhurkin; Production Specialist: Katy LaVigne

Image Credits
Alamy: Flight Plan, 70; DVIC: NARA, 9; Getty Images: American Stock, 60, claudiascheben, 88, Gamma-Keystone/Keystone-France, cover, 24, mb-fotos, 69, Popperfoto, 35, 100; The New York Public Library: 29; Newscom: Mirrorpix/Official, 105; Shutterstock: Borhax, 106, Dawid Lech, 46, Everett Collection, 6, 8, holwichaikawee (jail background), cover, back cover and throughout, Nik Merkulov (grunge background), 6 and throughout, Oliver Hoffmann, 22, Pixel62, 44, Simon Dux Media, 81, teddiviscious, 76; Superstock: age fotostock/Classic Vision, 17, Everett Collection, 10; U.S. Naval History and Heritage Command: 12, 38, 92; Wikimedia: 52, H.G. Durnford, 64

Printed and bound in China. 6274

CONTENTS

ABOUT YOUR ADVENTURE

YOU are an officer for the Allied forces during World War I (1914–1918). While bravely serving your country, you are captured behind enemy lines. Determined to fight another day, you hatch a daring plan to escape. Will you succeed and make your way to freedom?

Chapter One sets the scene. Then you choose which path to read. Follow the directions at the bottom of the page as you read the stories. The decisions you make will change your outcome. After you finish one path, go back and read the others for new perspectives and more adventures.

Turn the page to begin your adventure.

American soldiers fire a machine gun in the ragged ruins of a French forest in 1918.

CHAPTER 1

THE WORLD AT WAR

It's 1918, and the world has been in the grips of its first global war for four years. New technologies such as machine guns, tanks, fighter and bomber planes, and chemical weapons are used to inflict incredible carnage. It would be impossible to imagine the horrors if you hadn't seen so much of them yourself. People say this so-called Great War will be the war to end all wars. You can only hope it's true.

You are an officer on the side of the Allies. This group of countries includes Great Britain, Russia, France, Italy, Japan, and the United States. You're fighting against Germany, Austria-Hungary, Bulgaria, and the Ottoman Empire. This group of nations is known as the Central Powers.

Turn the page.

Deep trenches lined with sandbags provided soldiers fighting on the front lines with some protection from enemy fire.

The war is unfolding mainly on two fronts. On the Western Front, Germany invaded Belgium on its way to France—where Allied forces held them back. The two sides then dug trenches and now battle each other with artillery and machine guns. Neither side has gained or lost much ground for years, and the battles are extremely deadly. More than one million lives were lost in the Battle of the Somme in 1916. And that was just one battle.

At the same time, battle after battle rages on the Eastern Front. This is made up of the frontier between Russia and Romania on one side and Germany, Austria-Hungary, and other nations on the other.

Battles take place at sea and in the skies as well. German U-boats, or submarines, have been terrorizing the waters worldwide by sinking ships with torpedoes. They have targeted civilian and military vessels alike.

A German U-boat surfaces in the North Sea.

Turn the page.

French and German war planes engage in a dogfight.

And even though humans have only been able to fly for a few years, the Allies have already gained the upper hand in the air. They've used airplanes to gather information, for bombing runs, and for dogfights with enemy planes.

You've seen so much during the war. You've been a part of hard-won victories and terrifying retreats. You've seen friends killed in front of you.

You've also been scared more times than you can remember. But you face every challenge with courage. As an officer, it's expected of you. Never give in. Fight until the end.

So when you find yourself captured by the enemy, the fear is nothing new. You've been living with that for months. What is new is the quiet. A prison camp is far from the lines of battle. It's not peaceful, though. Oh no, far from that. It just reminds you that you're not fighting. You're not doing your part. And for that reason, you're desperate to escape and once again take the fight to the enemy.

You must escape or die trying.

To be an American Navy seaman captured by a German U-boat, turn to page 13.

To be a British fighter pilot in one of the worst prison camps in Germany, turn to page 47.

To be an American pilot captured during a bombing mission, turn to page 71.

The USS *President Lincoln* was a German ocean liner before being seized by the U.S. Navy to carry Allied troops and equipment to the Western Front.

CHAPTER 2
CAPTURED AT SEA

The United States tried to remain neutral in the Great War. For the first years, your country kept out of it. But as German U-boats sank more and more American ships, that became harder to do. Finally, in April 1917, the United States had had enough. It declared war on Germany.

You are fresh out of the Naval Academy by this time, and you are quickly deployed aboard a destroyer. That's where you live and work for the next several months. Life on the ship is cramped, busy, and nerve-wracking. U-boats can always be hiding beneath the dark waters, ready to strike.

Eventually you are transferred to the USS *President Lincoln*. It is an ocean liner that has been changed into a troop transport.

Turn the page.

On your first voyage aboard the ship, you meet Lieutenant Edouard Izac, the executive officer. He is second in command of the ship. You respect and admire the strong-willed, intelligent Izac, and he seems to appreciate you as well. You soon become friends. On your second voyage together, you successfully deliver troops from the United States to Brest, France.

For your return to the United States, your ship is joined by three other transports. All four are escorted by a destroyer. But the destroyer soon departs for another assignment, leaving the transports to sail alone.

"I don't like this," you say to Izac. The two of you are standing on the aft deck, near the big guns, watching the destroyer sail hastily away. Your uniforms flap wildly in the wind.

"It's not our job to like it," Izac says.

You both know it will be a dangerous voyage without the destroyer's protection, but Izac shows no fear. You have your orders, and you must obey them. A shiver goes up your spine, but it's not from the cold wind.

Sure enough, just after breakfast the next morning, two explosions rock the ship. Sailors scramble to their stations. You and Izac are stationed at the aft guns as usual when a third explosion hits. The ship shudders, and you are showered with water. Minutes later the telephone in your station rings, and you pick it up.

"The holds are flooding!" It's the captain. "Abandon ship!"

You and Izac escape in a lifeboat with a few sailors, and before long the *Lincoln* is gone. Sunk. But most of the crew has made it out alive. So that is good.

Turn the page.

You begin tying lifeboats together when a U-boat surfaces and approaches you. Seeing your officer stripes, the German captain takes you and Izac aboard the submarine. In English, he introduces himself as Captain Remy.

"Now," he says to you, "bring me to the captain of your ship."

There is no way you are going to help them find the captain, who right now is hiding his officer insignias under a blanket in one of the rafts. You also know that an American destroyer will be on its way to rescue you. You could tell them the captain went down with the ship so they stop looking for him. Or you could stall for time in hopes of being rescued by a destroyer.

To tell them the captain went down with the ship, go to page 17.

To stall for time, turn to page 19.

"Our captain is dead," you say, the wind lashing your face. You give Izac a knowing glance as the two of you stand on the deck of the U-boat.

"I do not believe you," Remy says.

"I wish it were not true," Izac says. "But he went down with the ship."

Remy waits for you to say more, but you and Izac say nothing. Soon the American destroyer is in sight, so you all go inside the submarine and Remy orders it to dive. You are brought into a small meeting room and left with two guards.

A cross-section reveals the tight quarters and cramped spaces below deck on a German U-boat.

Turn the page.

Outside the walls of the vessel, you hear the booming of depth charges fired from the destroyer. Then the two guards begin talking to each other in German. They are unaware that you speak German and can understand them.

"Will they send more destroyers?" one of them says.

"I hope they do not," says the other.

You know the United States will only spare one destroyer for this job. But perhaps you should tell them that more are coming from the direction you are heading. You might convince them to turn back toward the destroyer that really is there. You might get rescued. On the other hand, it might be useful to keep your ability to speak German a secret.

To tell them more destroyers are coming, turn to page 21.
To say nothing, turn to page 23.

To stall for time, you point to the lifeboat that is farthest away.

"I thought I saw him over there," you say.

Captain Remy orders the U-boat toward the other side of the group of lifeboats. It takes several minutes for the U-boat to reach the far lifeboat. They scan the men inside, but none of them is the captain.

"Maybe over there," Izac says, pointing to another raft in the distance.

Remy directs the U-boat in that direction. But when the captain is not there, his mouth pulls tight with anger and frustration.

"Do not try to fool me anymore," he says.

You are about to point him toward another lifeboat when you see an American destroyer on the horizon. It's moving swiftly toward you.

Turn the page.

"Inside," Remy commands.

You all go into the sub, and it dives beneath the surface. Soon, depth charges begin to explode in the water around you. Remy and his crew skillfully avoid the attack.

You sail for several days, and eventually you are transferred to a German destroyer. The destroyer takes you and Izac to land, and then you are transferred across many miles to a remote prison camp.

Immediately, you and Izac begin planning to escape. As you see it, there are two ways to go about this. You can try to bribe a guard for help. Or you can take a more direct route by climbing the high tree near the edge of the yard and leaping over the fence.

To try bribing a guard, turn to page 26.
To climb the tree, turn to page 28.

"Um, excuse me," you say in German. The two guards turn to you in confusion. "It is certain that at least one and possibly two more destroyers will be coming to hunt you down. They will likely be coming from the west where we have several ships stationed."

One of the guards leaves to report this news to Captain Remy. When he returns, he ignores you. It seems that Remy did not believe your lie. Worse, now they know that you understand German and will not speak freely around you anymore. This was a dumb mistake.

You sail on the submarine for several days. Because you are officers, you are treated fairly well. You have meals with the crew. They also give you freedom to move about the ship.

One night, you and Izac are up on the deck stretching your legs. Suddenly, you notice a faint shoreline not too far away.

Turn the page.

The coast of Denmark

Your heart skips a beat. You have been paying close attention to the direction the ship has been going. You realize that the land belongs to Denmark—a neutral country.

If you could make it there, you'd be free. You are already wearing a life preserver, but you also know the water will be freezing cold.

To jump overboard, turn to page 30.
To stay put, turn to page 32.

It's better not to let them know that you understand them, so you decide to say nothing.

The U-boat escapes the destroyer attack and sails for many days. Over time, the crew naturally begins to trust you a bit. They even let you keep your binoculars. Using them, you and Izac are able to figure out where you are.

Eventually, the ship arrives at a rendezvous point with other U-boats near Denmark—which are neutral waters where they can avoid Allied ships. You and Izac make a mental note of this location. It will be valuable to the Allies—if you can get away to tell them.

The next few weeks are a blur of travel. You are transferred to a German destroyer and then taken to two different prison camps in Germany. The second camp, located in the southern part of the country, is called Villingen.

Turn the page.

As you arrive by train, you notice Villingen is situated next to a river. You also notice a barracks for German soldiers right next to the camp. The camp and barracks are nestled in a thick forest. You pass through the gate in a nine-foot barbed wire fence, over a ditch filled with barbed wire, and through another barbed wire fence.

The opportunities for escape were few and far between while under the watchful eye of prison camp guards.

Over the next few weeks, a little news from the outside world trickles in. You learn that U-boats are sinking many American ships, and you are eager to escape and report the information you have learned. You could save American ships and lives.

One day you learn that all of the Russians in camp will be transferred elsewhere in a few days. That will leave only American prisoners. Izac worries that this will mean the guards can keep an even closer eye on the remaining prisoners.

"We need to get out before the Russians are moved," he tells you.

You have been thinking of building a ladder to escape. But you have not finished gathering your supplies or bribed the proper guards yet. You're just not ready.

To try to convince Izac to wait, turn to page 33.
To take your chances now, turn to page 35.

One of the guards you've met is not even German—he's Swiss. You know he was drafted into the German army and may not be very loyal. You stop him one night as he patrols the prisoners' rooms.

"Sir," you whisper.

He looks at you suspiciously, but he seems ready to listen. You say, "I have an offer for you."

You offer him American money and an escape from Germany. If you get out, you can arrange all of this. But you need his help.

The guard readily agrees. You wait anxiously over the next few days as he makes plans. Then, one afternoon, he catches you in the yard, yells at you, and knocks you to the ground. The other guards think nothing of this, which is ordinary behavior here. While you are down, he leans in close as if threatening you.

Instead, he says, "It is on for tomorrow night. I have sent a letter to my girlfriend. You will stay at her home. You will be safe there."

Unfortunately, the next day the guard is gone. In fact, you never see him again. Weeks later, you learn that his letter was intercepted by a German spy and he was taken away—probably to be killed.

Luckily, you avoid punishment because the commandant of the prison doesn't know the guard was helping you. Unfortunately, though, the guards are now watching everyone more closely than ever. A pit forms in your stomach as you realize you will probably spend the rest of the war in this awful place.

THE END

To read another adventure, turn to page 11.

To learn more about escapes during World War I, turn to page 101.

It almost seems too obvious, but you are sure it can work. Climb the tree and get away. It's perfect! You just have to wait for the guards to change shifts, leaving that corner of the yard unguarded for a moment. You've been watching, and it happens every night.

On the agreed-upon night, you and Izac sneak out the window of your room. Then you hide in the shadow of the building and wait. Unfortunately, the post below the tree is never left unguarded. For some reason, they are not following the same pattern they normally do. Eventually, you have no choice but to climb back into your room.

A few days later, the Germans put you on a train. You're being transferred to a different prison in the German countryside.

Captured French soldiers await transport by train in 1918.

Your best chance to escape is while in transit. Security is always tighter once you are in the camps. The guard next to you is snoozing. Izac nods to you and slowly, quietly opens his window. You realize he plans to jump from the moving train!

To jump out the window with Izac, turn to page 38.
To hold back, turn to page 40.

You give Izac the slightest nod, a signal that you want to jump. Captain Remy is only 20 paces away. You step toward the rail. You are almost close enough to jump.

Suddenly, Remy's voice rings out. "Stop!"

You and Izac freeze.

"Get inside," Remy says. His pistol is in his hand. "Go to your rooms."

Izac turns back. "What are you worried about?" he says to Remy, laughing. "It's too cold for a swim!"

Remy holsters his pistol. He laughs too. In that moment, you make a split-second decision: you jump.

You hit the water hard. It is icy cold, and you can feel it in your bones immediately.

You swim as hard as you can as gunshots rain down on you from above. You try to dive beneath the water, but your life preserver keeps you stuck on the surface. Suddenly, everything goes black. Are you freezing to death? Have you been shot? It doesn't matter. You're not going to make it to shore alive.

THE END

To read another adventure, turn to page 11.
To learn more about escapes during World War I,
turn to page 101.

It's just too risky to jump here. The water is so cold, you'd freeze before you made it the two or three miles to shore.

"Get away from that rail!" Remy yells at you. He's got his hand on his pistol. Another German nearby turns his machine gun toward you.

"Of course," you say. "Just admiring the view."

"I said get away!" Remy is clearly angry. "Get below deck."

After that, Remy doesn't seem to trust you any longer. He takes away your freedom to move around the boat. He takes away your binoculars. You are under constant supervision. There is no way you will be able to escape from this ship. You just hope you didn't waste your best chance.

THE END

To read another adventure, turn to page 11.
To learn more about escapes during World War I, turn to page 101.

"We're not ready!" you whisper to Izac in the dark. The two of you are lying in your hard beds under thin, scratchy blankets. "We need more time to gather supplies."

Izac waits a moment before responding. He says, simply, "I'm going."

Each of the next two nights, Izac meets a few other men behind your bunk building. On the third night, he doesn't return to bed. Suddenly, the lights in the camp cut out, and you hear chaos in the yard. Something clatters on the ground. You look out and see two men—neither is Izac—fumbling with a makeshift wooden ladder.

The next day, news spreads slowly among the prisoners that several men have escaped. Several men were also caught right away, and they are in solitary confinement. Izac is among the men who got away.

Turn the page.

The Russians are transferred later that week. Just as Izac guessed, the guards watch you more carefully than ever after that. Your only real chance to get away has passed.

THE END

To read another adventure, turn to page 11.
To learn more about escapes during World War I, turn to page 101.

Over the next few nights, you and Izac steal slats from wooden boxes that the Red Cross sends into camp with food and supplies. Izac also bribes a guard for a screwdriver so you can steal screws out of the prison's doors. Lastly, you steal two long boards from the tennis courts that are used to mark lines. You move your beds head-to-head and hide these boards beneath them.

After roll call one night, you and Izac screw together your ladder. The two tennis markers are the rails, and the box boards are the slats.

For prisoners looking to escape, the Red Cross's wooden boxes turned out to be just as valuable as the food and supplies they carried.

Turn the page.

At the agreed-upon time, other prisoners throw chains over some exposed wires to cut the lights in camp. Time to go! You extend the ladder out your window and across the yard to the outer wall. You have painted the bottom of the ladder with black shoe polish so that the guards won't notice it if they walk under.

It's a slow, clumsy trip across, but you make it. You drop over the far side of the wall and run into the woods. Later that night you meet two other Americans at the rendezvous spot, and you keep running. You can hear the howls and barks of dogs chasing you.

Close to morning, you hide in a crag in a cliff to catch a little sleep. The dogs bark and the guards call out well into the morning.

You have a choice. The Swiss border, and safety, is only 18 miles away. But the route is heavily patrolled by soldiers.

The other option is to go 120 miles through the mountains and the thickest part of the forest. There still will be patrols, but not nearly as many.

"I'm going the short way," one of the men whispers. "The long journey will be difficult without food or shelter."

But Izac says he is taking the long way because it's safer.

To go the short way, turn to page 41.
To go the long way, turn to page 43.

Lieutenant Edouard Izac

You nod in agreement, and he climbs head-first out the window and disappears. You cross the aisle and squeeze out after him.

You hit the ground and tuck into a ball, rolling away from the train and into a ravine. When you tumble to a stop, you hurt all over—but you don't think it's bad. You find Izac a hundred yards away. His legs and one arm are badly hurt.

SQUEAL! The train makes a braking sound. You know the soldiers will be after you very soon.

"I can't run," Izac says. "They're going to catch me. But you have a chance. You must go!"

You hesitate to leave him behind.

"Go! Now!" he yells again.

You take off into the woods. You hear the soldiers yelling, and then you hear Izac screaming in pain. They are beating him.

You keep running. Soon, there are gunshots. You realize it's hopeless. They will catch you—if they don't shoot you first.

THE END

To read another adventure, turn to page 11.
To learn more about escapes during World War I, turn to page 101.

You think jumping from a moving train is too dangerous. You shake your head to Izac that you shouldn't do it. But he shrugs his shoulders and turns to the window. In a flash, he is through it and out. You don't follow.

A guard starts yelling, and soon the train is braking. You sit and wait, hoping that Izac makes it. When the train stops, soldiers run out.

Within half an hour they return with Izac, who has been hurt in the fall and badly beaten by the Germans. You see them out the window. They force Izac to march the final 5 miles to the camp while the train goes on ahead.

The guards watch you more closely after that. You doubt you'll get a chance to escape now.

THE END

To read another adventure, turn to page 11.
To learn more about escapes during World War I, turn to page 101.

"The quicker the better," you say. "The longer we're out here, the more likely we'll get caught."

You try to convince Izac to join you and the other man. "We can be in Switzerland *by morning!*" you say.

But Izac sticks to his guns. "The long way is safer," he says.

That night, Izac and one of the men head into the woods. You and the other man walk on a road toward a small town. Every time you hear voices or steps, you hide in the woods. When you reach the town, you sneak through the dark streets. Every now and then you hear soldiers on patrol, and you hide.

At one point you see two soldiers who appear to be looking at you. You didn't hear them, and now you have no choice but to act casual and hope they think you are German citizens.

Turn the page.

You slowly turn around and walk away. But when one of the soldiers calls out in German, you break into a run. Suddenly, you hear footsteps on the next street over. You turn the other way—but as soon as you do, you are face-to-face with a soldier pointing a rifle right at you.

You raise your hands in the air. You know you're headed right back to prison—or worse.

THE END

To read another adventure, turn to page 11.

To learn more about escapes during World War I, turn to page 101.

At nightfall, you, Izac, and the other American make for the woods. You have a long journey ahead of you, so you walk several miles that night before stopping. You huddle together under Izac's overcoat. Light rain patters on the coat, and you barely sleep. After that you decide it's safe to travel by day.

By evening of the sixth day, you approach a town on the Rhine River. Switzerland lies on the other side. The three of you slip down to the bank and slather yourselves in mud.

As you make your way into the water, you slip on a rock and splash as you fall. Immediately, a searchlight ignites from the shore and is cast over the water. German voices bicker in the darkness. You all lie perfectly still, and the light passes over you. Then it turns off. The mud worked to make you blend in with the darkness. You just look like rocks in the river.

Turn the page.

The Rhine River on the border between Germany and Switzerland

You wait a few minutes to make sure no one is looking any longer. Then you stand up, shed your clothes, and dive into the rushing water. The current is strong, and you turn on your back and float. The river carries you, and eventually you feel rocks beneath your feet. You crawl to shore and catch your breath. You are in Switzerland!

When you don't see your friends, you get up and stumble to the hut of a nearby Swiss border guard. You tell the guard what happened, and he calls the Swiss military out to search the river bank. They return within the hour with Izac and the other American.

The three of you hug and laugh. You made it!

THE END

To read another adventure, turn to page 11.

To learn more about escapes during World War I, turn to page 101.

Both the Royal Flying Corps and the Royal Naval Air Service flew the Sopwith two-seater, designed as a high-performance fighter plane.

CHAPTER 3

ESCAPE FROM "HELLZMINDEN"

It is nearly dawn as you climb up into the cockpit of your Sopwith biplane. The base where you and your fellow British fighter pilots are stationed is about 20 miles from the battle front, but you can hear the shelling from here.

"Good morning, Jonesy!" you call to your gunner in the seat behind you. Then a mechanic yanks down on your propeller. You open the throttle, and the engine chokes to life. Blue smoke spews from the engine.

You pull on your goggles as you taxi your fighter plane to the runway. You begin to gather speed, and soon you are in the air. Several other planes join you on this dawn patrol.

Turn the page.

It's not long before you see German fighters on the horizon. You execute a couple tricky moves to avoid the fire of one of the Germans. Then you bank down toward another.

Jonesy opens fire. *Rat-tat-tat-tat!* It's a hit! The enemy's plane catches fire and goes down.

Suddenly, gunfire is unleashed on you from above. *Thunk-thunk-thunk!* Bullets smack into your engine casing. Smoke—thick black this time—spews from the compartment. You begin to lose altitude.

"Throw out the gun!" you yell to Jonesy. "The ammo too!"

Jonesy does as you say. Shedding that weight makes it easier to regain control of the plane. The engine is dead, but you glide toward a farm field. You land hard, crushing the crops and eventually coming to a stop near a stone wall.

Already, German soldiers are running across the field toward you. The soldiers are on you in minutes. They take you and Jonesy to separate prison camps. On your second night, you try to scale the wall—but the guards catch you just as you make it over.

The next day you are moved to Holzminden. It's a prison camp where they bring officers who have attempted to escape before. It is such a brutal place that it is known among the Allies by the nickname "Hellzminden." The commandant, Karl Niemeyer, taunts the prisoners by telling them that this place is escape-proof. This just makes you to want to escape even more.

A couple weeks later, another British pilot arrives at Holzminden and is assigned to your room. Scanlon is a daring and combative chap who has attempted five escapes already.

Turn the page.

You and Scanlon hit it off right away, and soon you agree to attempt an escape. The first thing you need to decide is whether to do it yourselves or bring in some other guys to help.

To do it yourselves, go to page 51.
To invite others into the plan, turn to page 52.

You both think it's too risky to open things up to more people. Every person who is part of the operation is a potential leak. Someone might rat you out to the guards in order to gain better treatment or better food. So you and Scanlon start planning on your own.

"Lots of trucks come in and out of here every day," Scanlon says.

It's true. Trucks deliver supplies such as laundry and food. They also transfer prisoners. If you could sneak into a truck, you might be able to ride—or drive—out and get far away before anyone notices. Then again, maybe you should make disguises before you try anything. Collecting materials and hiding them will be risky, but it could make things easier down the road.

To get out as soon as you can, turn to page 55.
To make disguises first, turn to page 57.

German guards and British prisoners stand outside and line the windows of the Block B building at Holzminden prison camp in 1918.

You are surrounded by officers, the best and brightest of the Allies. It just makes sense to utilize their intelligence and courage. Teaming up will give you the best chance to succeed.

You recruit a group of a couple dozen men. Then you, Scanlon, and the others size up the situation. The camp is surrounded by double walls and is patrolled by 100 guards. Many of them have attack dogs. With this in mind, you decide the only way to get out is to dig a tunnel.

You and the others take turns chiseling through a concrete wall beneath a stairwell in Block B. Then you bribe a civilian deliveryman to bring you some sulfuric acid. You use this to dissolve the iron bars in the concrete wall. After that, you've reached the dirt.

You steal a couple spoons and a bread knife from the meal commons and use these as tools. You set up a system where one man stands guard in the stairwell and one watches the guards out the window. The others take turns digging. It is slow, painstaking work. After a few weeks, you've dug dozens of feet. Then you run into a problem.

It's hard to breathe in there. The tunnel is barely wider than a crawling human body, and fresh air doesn't flow easily over the digger's body to his face. One of the men passes out in the tunnel and has to be dragged out to save his life. Some of the men are getting scared.

Turn the page.

"We need a bellows to pump in air," says one of the men.

"A bellows?" you say. "Sure, let's just ask the commandant. I'm sure he'll give us one."

But the other man is not joking. He says he can build one, but he'd need some materials. And it will take time—time that could be spent digging.

To just keep digging, turn to page 59.
To let him try to build a bellows, turn to page 60.

For the next two weeks, you and Scanlon carefully track the comings and goings of camp supply trucks. You note what days and times they arrive and how long they stay. You watch to see who the drivers talk to while here.

You note that the laundry truck driver always goes to the bathroom while the guards' dirty laundry is being loaded. The truck comes in the morning after head count but before breakfast. It's a time when you can move about the camp without being tracked carefully. You figure that's your best chance.

One morning after head count, you and Scanlon walk behind the bathhouse. The fresh laundry has already been unloaded, and the dirty laundry is being loaded. When the driver goes to the bathroom and the prisoners loading dirty laundry aren't looking, you jump into the back of the truck.

Turn the page.

You're climbing under some soiled sheets when you hear someone say, "Hey! Get out of there!"

It's one of the prisoners who does the loading. If you were to escape while he was on this job, he would be punished. He yells again, and suddenly there are several guards in the truck.

You're caught.

THE END

To read another adventure, turn to page 11.
To learn more about escapes during World War I, turn to page 101.

"Disguises," you say to Scanlon. "That's the best way. Once we get out, we can get farther if we don't attract attention to ourselves."

One day, Scanlon starts a fight in the yard. While the guards are distracted with that, you steal two jackets from the laundry.

Then Scanlon secures money from his family, which is smuggled in through the Red Cross. With that, he bribes a bread truck driver to bring in two caps. The driver also will let you sit in the truck with him as he drives out.

When the bread truck pulls in on the selected day, the driver sends the guard on duty to the back of the cookhouse for an empty bread crate. While the guard is gone, you and Scanlon climb into the truck with the coats and caps on.

The driver gets back in and drives to the gate. The guard glances up and waves you through.

Turn the page.

The driver stops about a mile from camp. You and Scanlon get out and begin walking. You look like German soldiers from a distance.

Unfortunately, you soon get stopped by a German patrol. You quickly find out your disguises don't work so well when someone sees you up close. The soldiers beat you severely and return you to Holzminden. You can only imagine what Commandant Niemeyer will do to you now.

THE END

To read another adventure, turn to page 11.
To learn more about escapes during World War I, turn to page 101.

Build a bellows? That's just too far-fetched to work. Besides, every day that passes is another chance you might be discovered. So the decision is made: keep digging.

But men keep passing out in the tunnel. Some say they are quitting because it's too dangerous.

Frustrated, you take more shifts digging. For whatever reason you last longer in there than most men. Every day you gain precious distance.

Then, one day, you pass out from lack of oxygen. Scanlon drags you out, and the next day you're at it again. Again, you feel your mind growing foggy. But this time, Scanlon can't get you out in time. As your eyes flutter shut, the tunnel goes dark for the final time.

THE END

To read another adventure, turn to page 11.
To learn more about escapes during World War I, turn to page 101.

"Let's give the bellows a shot," you say to the man, whose name is Gilligan.

You steal some lard from the kitchen, and several men steal tin cans from the garbage.

Gilligan uses his leather airman's jacket as the body of the bellows. He sews it up and uses the lard to seal the seams. He attaches the cans to one of the sleeves. Soon, the operation is underway again.

While one man is digging, another pumps the leather jacket open and shut. When it shuts, air is pumped along the tin cans, down the tunnel, to the man digging. It seems incredible, but the contraption actually works.

Meant for keeping airmen warm in an open cockpit, a leather jacket proved useful for building a bellows in Holzminden prison.

As the tunnel gets longer, you install stolen bed boards along the top to support it. Eventually, the tunnel is long enough to get beyond the camp's outer wall.

There is a field of rye just a hundred yards beyond the wall. The plan is for everyone to escape from the tunnel when the guards are passing on the other side of the compound. You should have just enough time to make a run for the rye, which is high enough to hide in.

Unfortunately, just as you are about to launch the escape, the commandant adds extra guards outside the walls. Now, they no longer circle the camp; they are stationed in place. It's just one guard and his dog. You might be able to outrun them. Then again, it may be safer to dig all the way to the rye, even if the escape has to wait.

To tunnel out to the original spot, turn to page 62.
To keep digging all the way to the rye, turn to page 64.

You believe you can catch the guard unaware. After all, who would expect someone to pop out of the ground behind them? You convince the men to go with your plan.

You take the bread knife and crawl through the tunnel. It's so tight that in some spots you can barely get through. Finally, you reach the end, and you start digging above you with the knife.

Soon, the first puff of fresh air comes in. You pause to catch your breath. There is no moon, so it's pitch dark. You push your arm through, then your head.

You lift yourself up to your waist and look around. The guard and his dog are by the wall looking out toward the prison's far corner. You hoist yourself up and start running. The prisoners behind you are waiting to see if you make it before they emerge.

You're almost to the rye when you hear the dog start barking. A flashlight splashes the ground around you. Suddenly, the dog is on your back, and you fall to the ground.

Although you realize you will probably die, you're more worried about the others. You hope they get the tunnel covered up before it is discovered. You hope they will still be able to get out.

THE END

To read another adventure, turn to page 11.
To learn more about escapes during World War I, turn to page 101.

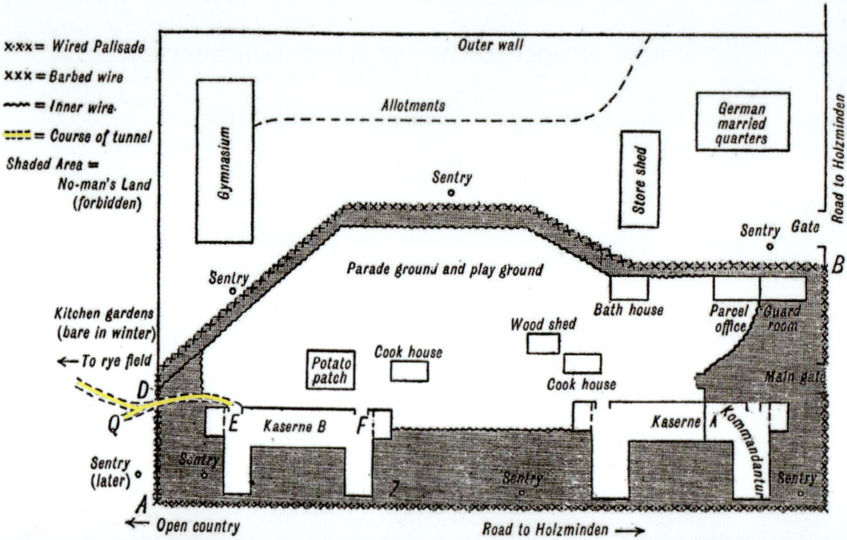

A map of Holzminden prison camp shows the path of the tunnel from Block B.

"We have no choice," you say. "We must tunnel to the rye. It's the only way."

Everyone's spirits are crushed. This will mean months more digging. But everyone agrees.

Many weeks later, you believe you are far enough. To test it, one of the men crawls through the tunnel with a white flag. When he gets to the end, he pokes the flag up through the ground.

You are watching from a window in Block B. To your horror, the flag pops out in the grass field. It seems as if the guard is looking right at it. Thankfully, he doesn't appear to notice.

The man with the flag returns, and you are forced to dig for another couple weeks. Finally you have dug far enough. You will come out of the tunnel in the field of rye, where nobody can see you.

Once you get out, you need a plan to make it to the Netherlands border. Most of the men plan to split up and travel alone or in groups of two. Their journeys will take weeks. But two of the other men speak German, and they plan to travel together and pass themselves off as Germans. They may be able to travel by train and reach the Netherlands much quicker.

To go it alone, turn to page 66.

To join the group, turn to page 68.

You don't speak German, and you don't want to blow everyone's cover. Besides, you feel confident you can do this on your own.

As one of the masterminds of the plan and someone who did a lot of the digging, you are one of the first to go in the tunnel. You inch slowly through it. It feels like it takes days, but finally you reach the end. You kick up and into the dark night. It is wonderful to be out!

You don't wait. You dash through the rye, into the woods, and on. The next few days you keep moving. You eat berries and pieces of bark. Using a compass that you'd hidden in the heel of your boot, you navigate toward the Netherlands border. You sleep little, and when you do sleep you have nightmares about tunneling.

One morning before dawn, you stop to get some rest. You slip into sleep and hear dogs barking. Is it a dream? It's hard to tell.

You try to wake yourself. You sit up and listen; all is quiet. If there were dogs, they're gone now. You shake your head to clear it. You must remain brave. Don't panic. Don't slow down. You've made it this far. You believe you will make it all the way.

THE END

To read another adventure, turn to page 11.

To learn more about escapes during World War I,
turn to page 101.

You are one of the first people to tunnel out. When you reach the end of the tunnel, you wait in the rye for your two companions, Blain and Kennard.

Once you are together, you walk to the first town, Bodenwerder. By following the road and going through towns, you should be able to reach the Netherlands in less than two weeks.

The plan is that Blain and Kennard are disguised as German doctors, and you pretend to be a patient who has escaped from a mental asylum. They are supposedly bringing you back. Your job is to act unstable. You hope it will cover up the fact that you don't speak German.

As you walk through Bodenwerder, you are thrilled to find that the plan is working perfectly. Citizens either ignore you or keep their distance out of an irrational fear of mental patients. The next town is Gellersen.

Gellersen, Germany

Here too, the plan works great. In this way, you make your way through a dozen German towns.

Eventually you arrive in Sellingen, which is on the border. As you cross over into the Netherlands, you let a big smile come over your face. For the first time in nearly two weeks, you break character. You are no longer a mental patient. You are yourself, and you are free.

THE END

To read another adventure, turn to page 11.
To learn more about escapes during World War I, turn to page 101.

The 96th Aero Squadron flew Breguet 14B.2 bombers. Their insignia, painted on the sides of their planes, showed a red devil holding a bomb.

CHAPTER 4
BOMBER PILOT

You are a bomber pilot in the 96th Aero Squadron, the first ever American day bombardment squad. You and your fellow pilots are very proud of this fact. You are stationed at an aerodrome in northeastern France, close to the front lines, where you live, train, and learn how to take care of the airplanes.

Your leader is Major Harry Brown. You believe he is a competent and inspiring leader, but he sometimes takes reckless chances. One day he orders the squadron to bomb some German railyards even though there is a vicious thunderstorm coming. The bad weather will make flying unsafe. Nevertheless, you obey your orders.

Turn the page.

You and the other pilots, including Brown, are flying in a V-formation into high winds. Fighting the winds uses lots of extra gas. Not only that, but it's hard to see as you are bobbing around in dense clouds. Before long, you get separated from your squadron. You are lost.

"Come in! Come in!" you bark into your radio. But there is no reply.

By now, you are dangerously low on fuel, and you have no choice but to land. You drop below the heavy clouds, but down here it's foggy. You can't tell where you are.

"I think we're in France somewhere," your bomber, Linden, suggests.

You land on a dirt road near a small village. You're barely out of the plane before a group of villagers comes up the road—and they are speaking German. You're behind enemy lines!

Your orders are to destroy your plane if in danger of being captured so that the enemy doesn't get their hands on it. But the villagers will be on you in a moment. They're not likely to be very friendly. A couple of them have rifles. Linden could fire his machine gun in the air to scare the villagers away. It might buy you enough time to destroy the plane. Then again, your best bet might be to simply run away.

To have Linden fire the machine gun, turn to page 74.
To run away, turn to page 77.

Linden fires over the heads of the villagers. As they flee, you scramble to set your maps on fire. You also smash the plane's instruments before dousing it in gasoline.

When the villagers return, they have German soldiers with them. Just as they arrive, you set the gasoline-soaked plane on fire.

The soldiers take your weapons and march you into the town. You wait outside an office while the officer in charge makes a phone call. Soon, a truck pulls up and you are loaded inside.

They drive you through the countryside to an old fortress across the street from a small village. The fortress is called Friedrichsfeste. It's a two-story building with bars on the windows and thick steel doors. As you approach, you realize this fortress has been transformed into a prison. This will be your home until the end of the war—or until you can escape.

At night, you and Linden lie in your hard, uncomfortable beds and listen to the guards patrolling outside the building. You endure many surprise room inspections, making it impossible to collect anything to help in an escape.

But after a couple weeks, one of the prisoners tells you a window in one of the rooms has a loose bar. Some French prisoners had removed it some time ago and replaced it so it *looks* secure.

Linden has had a terrible flu, but you decide not to wait. That night, the two of you tie your sheets together end to end and go to the room with the loose bar. The guard below circles the building. When he turns the corner, you drop the line and shimmy down.

You hide in some tall grass as the guard comes around again, your heart racing with fear. Again, he disappears around the corner—and you dash for the little village.

Turn the page.

You try to move through the village quickly but casually, as if you belong there. You stroll past someone standing in his garden who says "hello" in German. Neither you nor Linden speak German, so you respond with a grunt and keep walking. You glance back and notice the man watching you.

To start running, turn to page 79.
To keep it casual, turn to page 80.

"Let's get out of here, Linden!" you shout.

You run across the field, and one of the villagers fires a rifle. In seconds, you're out of the field and into the trees. You keep running into the night. Unfortunately, German soldiers catch up with you within three days.

You are transferred to an old hotel in the town of Karlsruhe. An intelligence officer grills you for information about your mission. But you are well-trained, and you reveal nothing. After several hours, the guards put you in a room with Linden and four other prisoners.

"Enjoy your accommodations," one of the guards says sarcastically. "In a few days, you will be transferred to your permanent prison."

Two of the other prisoners are Frenchmen, and the other two are English. At first, all six of you are nervous and keep to yourselves.

Turn the page.

But soon, one of the Englishmen starts chatting. He complains about the food here, and everyone agrees. He says he misses his family, and everyone agrees they miss theirs too. As you all get to know one another, you start to relax.

On the second morning, the chatty Englishman starts talking about his mission and how he got captured. He gives details of where he came from and what he was after.

"Top secret recon," he concludes.

Information like this is classified, and the Englishman should not be talking about it—even with allies. Of course, you're all trapped together. What harm could come?

Then the Englishman turns to you. "What about you, mate?" he says.

To talk about your mission, turn to page 82.
To keep quiet, turn to page 84.

"He's still watching us," you whisper to Linden.

"I don't like this," he whispers back.

"Let's get out of here," you say.

You and Linden break into a run, your boots clattering on the cobblestone street. The man in the garden begins yelling in German, and you turn a corner to get out of his sight.

But his yelling alerts others in the village. Men and women come out of their homes on every block. Some of them have weapons. Guards from the prison are alerted now too.

You make it through the town to the countryside, but it's useless. It's only a matter of time before you're caught.

THE END

To read another adventure, turn to page 11.

To learn more about escapes during World War I, turn to page 101.

"Just keep walking," you say.

Calmly, you turn down the next street to get out of his view. Then you turn again. You walk through the small village and into the nearby countryside. Once there, you run. Soon you are safely in the Black Forest.

You work your way through the forest for the next several nights, laying low during the day and avoiding towns. The weather turns rainy and cold, and your thin clothes become soaked.

In an effort to make better time, you start taking some chances. On two different nights, you walk on a road instead of in the woods. You make many miles, and nobody sees you.

When you reach the town of Neustadt, you're exhausted. Linden was already sick before you left, and now he's stumbling as he walks. You need to get to the safety of France, and soon.

Neustadt is nestled in the south of Germany's Black Forest region.

Neustadt is one of the biggest towns in the forest. Going around it will take a very long time but might be safer. If you go straight through, you could save a couple days of travel time. You've gotten away with your gambles so far.

To walk through the town, turn to page 86.
To stick to the woods, turn to page 88.

Something about being trapped with all these men has given you a sense of brotherhood with them. You think it's okay to reveal just a little of your mission.

"We were on our way to bomb a railyard near Koblenz," you say.

"The railyards, eh?" the Englishman says. He asks where your base is, and you tell him. Then he asks a few more questions. Finally, Linden nudges you with his elbow, and you understand. Perhaps you can't trust this guy after all.

Later that day, the Englishman is pulled out of the room by the guards. The rest of you are left behind.

"Well that confirms it," Linden says to you. "They pulled him out because his job is done. He's a spy!"

Linden is furious with you. The Frenchmen just shake their heads.

You are kept here for another week before you are transferred to a POW camp deep in the forest next to an infantry barracks. Some of the men are planning an escape. But they don't trust you after your mistake back at the "Listening Hotel," and they do not invite you into their plan.

THE END

To read another adventure, turn to page 11.
To learn more about escapes during World War I, turn to page 101.

You don't trust this guy. Linden becomes suspicious and starts hunting around the room. Sure enough, he finds a microphone hidden in the lamp.

"The only reason they brought us here is to spy on us," Linden says.

He turns to the Englishman and is about to fight him when the door opens. The guards remove the Englishman from the room, confirming your suspicions. He was a spy.

The Germans realize they will not get any information from you here at the "Listening Hotel." It's not long before they transfer you to a prison called Villingen in southern Germany.

At Villingen, you and Linden quickly make friends with other prisoners, all of whom are officers like you. One of them is Major Brown, your leader from the 96th.

You soon learn Brown made an emergency landing of his own and was captured after nine days on the run. You are glad to see him alive.

Talking to Brown and other men, you learn of a plot to escape. Several teams of men have already been at work. They've built ladders, which will be key to the escape. There is room for you and Linden on one of two teams. One is led by Major Brown. The other is led by an American ambulance driver named Harold Willis. You barely know Willis, but he seems confident and capable.

To stick with Major Brown, turn to page 90.
To throw in with Willis, turn to page 92.

"We need to get you to a hospital as soon as possible," you say to Linden. "We're going to have to take a chance with the town."

Late that night, you walk through the edge of the town. All is quiet. Occasionally you see the curtains move in a house. People hear your boots on the road and look to see who is out there at this hour.

When you pass a small home with a garden, you stop to pick tomatoes and peppers. It is amazing to taste good, fresh food after so long.

You and Linden are just standing there smiling—red tomato juice pouring off your chins—when you hear boots clacking in the road. That's the sound of soldiers approaching!

"Someone's coming!" Linden exclaims. "What do we do?

"Quick, get into the garden," you reply.

You both crawl into the garden and hide behind a shrub, but it is no use. A flashlight shines over the bush into your eyes. Then a voice says, in English, "Come out of there now!"

Your heart sinks knowing you're headed right back to prison.

THE END

To read another adventure, turn to page 11.

To learn more about escapes during World War I, turn to page 101.

For the next three days, you stick to the woods and continue your pattern. You walk at night and rest during the day. Occasionally you find berries, but there just isn't enough food. Linden is getting sicker, and you are starting to feel weak too. By the sixth night, Linden cannot get up to walk.

"It's all right," you say, hoping to make him feel better. "We'll just rest a day or two."

You search the area and find some acorns and walnuts. The food helps, but not much. Finally, you set out once again.

Wild blueberries growing in the Black Forest

Unfortunately, now you are sick too. You have a fever. You must be in bad shape, because you don't even hear the German soldier who has been trailing you. When he steps out of the shadows with his rifle pointed at you, you're so sick you're almost relieved to be caught.

THE END

To read another adventure, turn to page 11.

To learn more about escapes during World War I, turn to page 101.

Major Brown is your superior, and you feel that you must join him. On the night of the escape, several other prisoners execute a plan to cut the lights in the yard. On cue, you slide the ladder out your window and climb down. Other teams are using their ladders as a bridge from their windows all the way to the outer wall. Your plan is to get down out of the room, carry the ladder across the yard, and scale the outer wall. You can see Willis's team already at the outer wall.

Brown is just reaching the ground when he stumbles and catches his foot on the ladder. It drops to the ground, clattering loudly.

Linden and the fourth man are still up in the window. You've wasted precious time, and you don't know if the noise has attracted attention. Meanwhile, the guards are heading to the light towers to see what's wrong there.

Your heart races as you look up to Linden in the window.

"We have to leave them!" Brown whispers. "We'll never make it if we don't go *now!*"

To leave them behind, turn to page 94.
To go back for them, turn to page 96.

Americans Harold Willis (center) and Edouard Izac (right), along with two British officers, at Villingen prison camp in 1918

You have seen Brown make mistakes in the past. You'd rather try your luck with Willis.

Two nights later, you, Willis, Linden, and another man are crouched in one of the rooms, waiting. One advantage of being on Willis's team is that he has disguises that make you look like German guards.

At the appointed time, the lights go out, just as planned. You quickly extend your ladder out the window and the four of you climb down.

Once you reach the ground, you approach the guards' compound. An alarm is going off, and the doors to the compound are open. Guards come out yawning, still buttoning their uniforms. A sergeant yells orders. You step into the gaggle of guards and try to act natural.

Some of the guards go to the main gate, and one works to get it open. Willis follows them.

But Linden looks nervous. He makes eye contact with one of the guards, and you can see panic in his eyes. He begins moving with the group heading toward the cell block.

You realize Linden is going to try to get back into his room to avoid being caught. You have to make a split-second decision—go back with Linden or continue on with Willis.

To go back with Linden, turn to page 97.
To continue on with Willis, turn to page 98.

Your only hope is to go for it now. You and Brown carry your ladder to the wall and quickly scramble up.

At the top of the wall, you take a brief look back at Linden in the window. He gives you a little wave. You feel bad, but it was the only choice you had, really.

You jump down the other side and begin to run. Unfortunately, you lost a lot of time fiddling with the ladder, and the guards are close behind you. You are captured within the hour and severely beaten.

Back in the prison, you are placed in solitary confinement for two weeks. Your injuries are so bad, and you feel so confused from the lack of light or human contact, that eventually you don't know if you're living or dead.

But you still know one thing for sure: You will spend the rest of the war in this prison, if you don't die here before it's over.

THE END

To read another adventure, turn to page 11.

To learn more about escapes during World War I, turn to page 101.

You're not going to leave Linden behind. You grab the ladder from Brown and prop it on the wall. You wave Linden down, but he shakes his head. "It's too late!" he says.

You can hear the commotion getting louder, and you realize he's right. Guards will be coming. Your only hope is to get back inside and pretend you didn't have anything to do with the escape.

You climb up as quickly as you can, with Brown right behind you. You pull in the ladder just as guards round the corner. Linden hides it in one of the rooms of the men who escaped.

You won't get out this time. But now you know it can be done—perhaps with a more competent leader.

THE END

To read another adventure, turn to page 11.
To learn more about escapes during World War I, turn to page 101.

You stick close to Linden in the crowd of guards moving toward the housing unit. When you get close, you break away from the group. It's only then that you realize the foolishness of your decision. As you turn the corner toward your window, you see that the ladder has already been taken down by the guards. With the doors locked, you have no way to get back to your room.

You turn in desperation to run after Willis, but he's long gone. Still, you make your way toward the gate. But just before you reach it, some guards slam it shut. It's only a matter of time now before you are discovered.

THE END

To read another adventure, turn to page 11.
To learn more about escapes during World War I, turn to page 101.

You're not giving up now. You and Willis reach the gate and nervously wait for it to be unlocked. The guards are no longer sleepy. They are fired up to catch the escaping prisoners. They're yelling and shaking their fists in the air, scanning the land outside the gates.

A couple prisoners drop off the wall and scramble into the woods. Finally, the gate is unlocked, and the guards rush after the escapees.

While most of the guards give chase, you and Willis edge away from the group. You head for the road. You've made it maybe 50 yards when you hear a guard behind you yell something.

You don't turn to see if it's you he's yelling after; you just run for the woods. There are gunshots, but again, you don't bother to find out if they are intended for you. Your only thoughts are on getting as far away as you can as fast as you can.

You scramble through the brush and trees. Two hours later, you meet up with a fellow escapee—an American Navy lieutenant—at an agreed-upon spot. The three of you run through the night.

You have a long journey ahead of you. Your best chance is to make it to Switzerland, a neutral country that will give you safety. But with Willis at your side, you know you will make it.

THE END

To read another adventure, turn to page 11.
To learn more about escapes during World War I, turn to page 101.

Russian prisoners of war at a German prison camp during World War I

CHAPTER 5

DARING ESCAPES OF WORLD WAR I

Prisoner-of-war camps were common during World War I and were used by both the Allies and the Central Powers. Russia had more than 400 facilities that held about 2.4 million prisoners by the end of the war, most of whom were Austro-Hungarian. Hundreds of thousands of men were held in Great Britain, with the majority of them being German. The United States, which was only in the war for about a year and a half and was not near the battle fronts, held just over 4,000 German prisoners. For its part, Germany held about 2.4 million prisoners during the war in nearly 300 camps.

When captured, soldiers were usually separated into camps for officers and camps for enlisted men. Conditions in camps varied widely, but in general, officers were treated much better than enlisted men. They had better food and more comfortable living conditions. As a result, imprisoned officers were typically healthier and better equipped to escape than enlisted men. Not only that, but officers often felt it was their duty to try to escape. In fact, the only known successful escape attempts were pulled off by officers.

The escapes in this book are based on real events, and some of the characters were real people. Lieutenant Izac was captured after the USS *President Lincoln* was sunk by a German U-boat. On the sub, he secretly listened to the German sailors. While being transferred to Villingen prison, he jumped out of a moving train but was badly hurt and recaptured.

Once at Villingen, Izac met several other officers, including a fighter pilot named Sergeant Harold Willis. Together they planned the escape using cobbled-together ladders. Though Izac and Willis took different paths out of the camp, they met up after breaking out. Then they traveled together through the Black Forest to the Rhine River, which they crossed into Switzerland.

Many captured soldiers spent a few days or weeks at a converted hotel near Karlsruhe, Germany. This location was specifically set up for spying. Microphones were hidden in the rooms in the hopes that Allied soldiers would talk about their missions or other secret things.

Sometimes the Germans sent spies into the rooms. These men pretended to be Allied prisoners and asked the other captives questions designed to get precious information. The hotel came to be nicknamed the "Listening Hotel."

Holzminden prison camp was the site of one of the most dramatic and famous escapes in history. Many officer prisoners had attempted to escape in different ways, from disguising themselves and walking out to cutting the fence. Many succeeded in getting out, but nearly all of them were recaptured within days.

The only successful attempt was by those who tunneled out. Dozens of officers participated in the operation, taking turns digging and acting as lookouts over the course of months.

Just when they thought they had tunneled to a field of rye that would give them cover, Commandant Niemeyer added extra guards outside the camp. This meant the prisoners had to tunnel farther—and for more weeks—than they had planned. A makeshift bellows made from a leather jacket and tin cans was key to keeping the diggers breathing while deep inside.

Cecil Blain (left), David Gray (center), and Caspar Kennard were just three of 10 prisoners to reach freedom after the daring Holzminden tunnel escape.

Of the 86 officers who tried to get out, only 29 made it. That's because the tunnel collapsed in spite of the bed boards they had used to sturdy it. The 30th man was trapped inside. Unfortunately, most of the escaped prisoners were recaptured. But 10 succeeded in making it to safety in the Netherlands.

KEY LOCATIONS OF THE ESCAPES

KEY EVENTS OF WORLD WAR I

JULY 28, 1914 Austria-Hungary declares war on Serbia, beginning the war.

AUGUST 1–30, 1914 The war escalates after Germany invades Luxembourg and Belgium, France invades Alsace, and Austria-Hungary invades Russia.

MAY 23, 1915 Italy declares war on Austria-Hungary, joining the war on the side of the Allies.

APRIL 6, 1917 The United States enters the war on the side of the Allies by declaring war on Germany.

AUGUST 18, 1917 Sergeant Harold Willis is shot down and captured by Germans.

MAY 31, 1918 The USS *President Lincoln* is sunk, and Lieutenant Edouard Izac is taken prisoner.

JULY 23, 1918 Twenty-nine Allied prisoners escape from Holzminden prison camp in Germany.

OCTOBER 6, 1918 Izac and Willis escape from Villingen prison and reach the Swiss border six days later.

NOVEMBER 11, 1918 Germany signs the armistice, ending the war.

OTHER PATHS TO EXPLORE

- Enlisted Allied soldiers who were captured behind enemy lines were not treated as well as officers. What would it have been like to attempt an escape from a prison camp as an enlisted soldier?

- Airplanes were relatively new technology during World War I and often broke down. Imagine you are a pilot who crash lands behind enemy lines but avoids immediate capture. How would you make your way back to your own side?

- World War I infantry soldiers often lived and fought in long, deep trenches running parallel with the enemy's trenches. The space between the trenches was called "no man's land." Imagine you are a soldier who gets trapped in no man's land. How would you make your way back to your side's trench?

GLOSSARY

aerodrome (AIR-oh-drome)—a small airport or airfield

aft (AFT)—the rear part of a ship or boat

Allies (AL-lyz)—a group of countries that fought together in World War I; the Allies included the United States, Great Britain, France, Russia, Italy, and Japan

bellows (BELL-ohs)—a device with an air bag that pumps a stream of air when squeezed

biplane (BYE-plane)—an airplane with two sets of wings, one above the other, flown in the early 1900s

Central Powers (SEN-truhl PAU-uhrs)—a group of countries that fought the Allies in World War I; the Central Powers included Germany, Austria-Hungary, Bulgaria, and the Ottoman Empire

depth charge (DEPTH CHARJ)—a metal can filled with explosives that is dropped into water and sinks to a specific depth before exploding

destroyer (di-STROI-ur)—a small, fast warship that is equipped to fight submarines and aircraft

officer (OF-uh-sur)—someone in the military who is in charge of other people

rendezvous (RON-deh-voo)—a French word meaning a meeting at an agreed-upon time and place

BIBLIOGRAPHY

Bascomb, Neal. *The Escape Artists*. New York: Mariner Books, 2018.

Harper, Kris Cotariu. "Lieutenant Edouard V. Izac, the Last Surviving Medal of Honor Recipient from WWI." Congressional Medal of Honor Society. May 31, 2021. cmohs.org/news-events/medal-of-honor-recipient-profile/lieutenant-edouard-v-izac-the-last-surviving-medal-of-honor-recipient-from-wwi.

History.com: World War I. February 22, 2023. history.com/topics/world-war-i/world-war-i-history.

Lloyd, Keith Warren. *The Greatest POW Escape Stories Ever Told*. Guilford, CT: Lyons Press, 2020.

Messimer, Dwight R. *Escape from Villingen, 1918*. College Station, TX: Texas A&M University Press, 2000.

Mikaelian, Allen. *Medal of Honor*. New York: Hyperion, 2002.

READ MORE

Doeden, Matt. *Can You Survive a World War II Escape? An Interactive History Adventure.* North Mankato, MN: Capstone Press, 2024.

Medina, Nico. *What Was World War I?* New York: Penguin Workshop, 2023.

Monroe, Alex. *World War I.* Minneapolis: Bellwether Media, Inc., 2024.

INTERNET SITES

DK Findout!: World War I
dkfindout.com/us/history/world-war-i

National Geographic Kids: World War I Facts
natgeokids.com/uk/discover/history/general-history/first-world-war

The National World War I Museum and Memorial
theworldwar.org

ABOUT THE AUTHOR

photo by Jeff Wheeler

Eric Braun is a children's author and editor. He has written dozens of books on many topics, and one of his books was read by an astronaut on the International Space Station for kids on Earth to watch. Eric lives in Minneapolis, Minnesota, with his wife, two kids, and a dog who is afraid of cardboard.

BOOKS IN THIS SERIES